Diving into the Wreck

By Adrienne Rich

Of Woman Born: Motherhood as Experience and Institution
Poems: Selected and New, 1950–1974
Diving into the Wreck
The Will to Change
Leaflets
Necessities of Life
Snapshots of a Daughter-in-Law
The Diamond Cutters and Other Poems
A Change of World

ADRIENNE RICH

Diving into
the Wreck

Poems 1971–1972

W · W · NORTON & COMPANY · INC ·

NEW YORK

Many of these poems first appeared in the following periodicals: *American Poetry Review, The American Review, Antaeus, Aphra, Equal Time, Field, Mulberry, The Nation, The New York Review of Books, Ohio Review, Partisan Review, Place, Ramparts, Salmagundi, Saturday Review, The Second Wave, Unmuzzled Ox, Women's Studies.*

Copyright © 1973 by W. W. Norton & Company, Inc.

Library of Congress Cataloging in Publication Data

Diving into the wreck.
I. Title.
PS3535.I233D58   811'.5'4   73–2626
ISBN 0–393–04370–3
ISBN 0–393–04384–3 (pbk)

Book Designer: Robert Freese

PRINTED IN THE UNITED STATES OF AMERICA

Contents

IV

I

Perhaps my life is nothing but an image of this kind; perhaps I am doomed to retrace my steps under the illusion that I am exploring, doomed to try and learn what I should simply recognize, learning a mere fraction of what I have forgotten.
—*André Breton,* Nadja

There is no private life which is not determined by a wider public life.
—*George Eliot*

Trying to Talk with a Man

Out in this desert we are testing bombs,

that's why we came here.

Sometimes I feel an underground river
forcing its way between deformed cliffs
an acute angle of understanding
moving itself like a locus of the sun
into this condemned scenery.

What we've had to give up to get here—
whole LP collections, films we starred in
playing in the neighborhoods, bakery windows
full of dry, chocolate-filled Jewish cookies,
the language of love-letters, of suicide notes,
afternoons on the riverbank
pretending to be children

Coming out to this desert
we meant to change the face of
driving among dull green succulents
walking at noon in the ghost town
surrounded by a silence

that sounds like the silence of the place
except that it came with us
and is familiar
and everything we were saying until now
was an effort to blot it out—
Coming out here we are up against it

Out here I feel more helpless
with you than without you
You mention the danger

and list the equipment
we talk of people caring for each other
in emergencies—laceration, thirst—
but you look at me like an emergency

Your dry heat feels like power
your eyes are stars of a different magnitude
they reflect lights that spell out: EXIT
when you get up and pace the floor

talking of the danger
as if it were not ourselves
as if we were testing anything else.

1971

When We Dead Awaken

(*for E. Y.*

1.   Trying to tell you how
the anatomy of the park
through stained panes, the way
guerrillas are advancing
through minefields, the trash
burning endlessly in the dump
to return to heaven like a stain—
everything outside our skins is an image
of this affliction:
stones on my table, carried by hand
from scenes I trusted
souvenirs of what I once described
as happiness
everything outside my skin
speaks of the fault that sends me limping
even the scars of my decisions
even the sunblaze in the mica-vein
even you, fellow-creature, sister,
sitting across from me, dark with love,
working like me to pick apart
working with me to remake
this trailing knitted thing, this cloth of darkness,
this woman's garment, trying to save the skein.

2.   The fact of being separate
enters your livelihood like a piece of furniture
—a chest of seventeenth-century wood

from somewhere in the North.
It has a huge lock shaped like a woman's head
but the key has not been found.
In the compartments are other keys
to lost doors, an eye of glass.
Slowly you begin to add
things of your own.
You come and go reflected in its panels.
You give up keeping track of anniversaries,
you begin to write in your diaries
more honestly than ever.

3.   The lovely landscape of southern Ohio
     betrayed by strip mining, the
     thick gold band on the adulterer's finger
     the blurred programs of the offshore pirate station
     are causes for hesitation.
     Here in the matrix of need and anger, the
     disproof of what we thought possible
     failures of medication
     doubts of another's existence
     —tell it over and over, the words
     get thick with unmeaning—
     yet never have we been closer to the truth
     of the lies we were living, listen to me:
     the faithfulness I can imagine would be a weed
     flowering in tar, a blue energy piercing
     the massed atoms of a bedrock disbelief.

1971

6

Waking in the Dark

1.

The thing that arrests me is

    how we are composed of molecules

    (he showed me the figure in the paving stones)

    arranged without our knowledge and consent

        like the wirephoto composed
        of millions of dots

        in which the man from Bangladesh
        walks starving

            on the front page
            knowing nothing about it

        which is his presence for the world

2.

We were standing in line outside of something
two by two, or alone in pairs, or simply alone,
looking into windows full of scissors,
windows full of shoes. The street was closing,
the city was closing, would we be the lucky ones
to make it? They were showing
in a glass case, the Man Without A Country.
We held up our passports in his face, we wept for him.

They are dumping animal blood into the sea
to bring up the sharks. Sometimes every
aperture of my body
leaks blood. I don't know whether
to pretend that this is natural.

7

Is there a law about this, a law of nature?
You worship the blood
you call it hysterical bleeding
you want to drink it like milk
you dip your finger into it and write
you faint at the smell of it
you dream of dumping me into the sea.

3.

The tragedy of sex
lies around us, a woodlot
the axes are sharpened for.
The old shelters and huts
stare through the clearing with a certain resolution
—the hermit's cabin, the hunters' shack—
scenes of masturbation
and dirty jokes.
A man's world. But finished.
They themselves have sold it to the machines.
I walk the unconscious forest,
a woman dressed in old army fatigues
that have shrunk to fit her, I am lost
at moments, I feel dazed
by the sun pawing between the trees,
cold in the bog and lichen of the thicket.
Nothing will save this. I am alone,
kicking the last rotting logs
with their strange smell of life, not death,
wondering what on earth it all might have become.

4.

Clarity,

      spray

blinding and purging

spears of sun striking the water

the bodies riding the air

like gliders

the bodies in slow motion

falling

into the pool

at the Berlin Olympics

control; loss of control

the bodies rising

arching back to the tower

time reeling backward

clarity of open air

before the dark chambers

with the shower-heads

the bodies falling again

freely

              faster than light

the water opening

like air

like realization

A woman made this film

against

the law

of gravity

5.

All night dreaming of a body
space weighs on differently from mine
We are making love in the street
the traffic flows off from us
pouring back like a sheet
the asphalt stirs with tenderness
there is no dismay
we move together like underwater plants

Over and over, starting to wake
I dive back to discover you
still whispering, *touch me,* we go on
streaming through the slow
citylight forest ocean
stirring our body hair

But this is the saying of a dream
on waking
I wish there were somewhere
actual we could stand
handing the power-glasses back and forth
looking at the earth, the wildwood
where the split began

1971

Incipience

1. To live, to lie awake
under scarred plaster
while ice is forming over the earth
at an hour when nothing can be done
to further any decision

to know the composing of the thread
inside the spider's body
first atoms of the web
visible tomorrow

to feel the fiery future
of every matchstick in the kitchen

Nothing can be done
but by inches. I write out my life
hour by hour, word by word
gazing into the anger of old women on the bus
numbering the striations
of air inside the ice cube
imagining the existence
of something uncreated
this poem
our lives

2. A man is asleep in the next room
We are his dreams
We have the heads and breasts of women
the bodies of birds of prey
Sometimes we turn into silver serpents

While we sit up smoking and talking of how to live
he turns on the bed and murmurs

A man is asleep in the next room
     A neurosurgeon enters his dream
     and begins to dissect his brain
     She does not look like a nurse
     she is absorbed in her work
     she has a stern, delicate face like Marie Curie
She is not/might be either of us

A man is asleep in the next room
     He has spent a whole day
     standing, throwing stones into the black pool
     which keeps its blackness
Outside the frame of his dream we are stumbling up the hill
     hand in hand, stumbling and guiding each other
     over the scarred volcanic rock

1971

After Twenty Years

(*for A. P. C.*

Two women sit at a table by a window. Light breaks
unevenly on both of them.
Their talk is a striking of sparks
which passers-by in the street observe
as a glitter in the glass of that window.
Two women in the prime of life.
Their babies are old enough to have babies.
Loneliness has been part of their story for twenty years,
the dark edge of the clever tongue,
the obscure underside of the imagination.
It is snow and thunder in the street.
While they speak the lightning flashes purple.
It is strange to be so many women,
eating and drinking at the same table,
those who bathed their children in the same basin
who kept their secrets from each other
walked the floors of their lives in separate rooms
and flow into history now as the woman of their time
living in the prime of life
as in a city where nothing is forbidden
and nothing permanent.

1971

The Mirror in Which
Two Are Seen As One

1.

She is the one you call sister.
Her simplest act has glamor,
as when she scales a fish the knife
flashes in her long fingers
no motion wasted or when
rapidly talking of love
she steel-wool burnishes
the battered kettle

Love-apples cramp you sideways
with sudden emptiness
the cereals glutting you, the grains
ripe clusters picked by hand
Love: the refrigerator
with open door
the ripe steaks bleeding
their hearts out in plastic film
the whipped butter, the apricots
the sour leftovers

A crate is waiting in the orchard
for you to fill it
your hands are raw with scraping
the sharp bark, the thorns
of this succulent tree
Pick, pick, pick
this harvest is a failure
the juice runs down your cheekbones
like sweat or tears

2.

She is the one you call sister
you blaze like lightning about the room
flicker around her like fire
dazzle yourself in her wide eyes
listing her unfelt needs
thrusting the tenets of your life
into her hands

She moves through a world of India print
her body dappled
with softness, the paisley swells at her hip
walking the street in her cotton shift
buying fresh figs because you love them
photographing the ghetto because you took her there

Why are you crying dry up your tears
we are sisters
words fail you in the stare of her hunger
you hand her another book
scored by your pencil
you hand her a record
of two flutes in India reciting

3.

Late summer night the insects
fry in the yellowed lightglobe
your skin burns gold in its light
In this mirror, who are you? Dreams of the nunnery
with its discipline, the nursery
with its nurse, the hospital
where all the powerful ones are masked
the graveyard where you sit on the graves
of women who died in childbirth
and women who died at birth

Dreams of your sister's birth
your mother dying in childbirth over and over
not knowing how to stop
bearing you over and over

your mother dead and you unborn
your two hands grasping your head
drawing it down against the blade of life
your nerves the nerves of a midwife
learning her trade

1971

From the Prison House

Underneath my lids another eye has opened
it looks nakedly
at the light

that soaks in from the world of pain
even when I sleep

Steadily it regards
everything I am going through

and more

it sees the clubs and rifle-butts
rising and falling
it sees

detail not on TV

the fingers of the policewoman
searching the cunt of the young prostitute
it sees

the roaches dropping into the pan
where they cook the pork
in the House of D

it sees
the violence
embedded in silence

This eye
is not for weeping
its vision
must be unblurred

though tears are on my face

its intent is clarity
it must forget
nothing

September 1971

The Stranger

Looking as I've looked before, straight down the heart
of the street to the river
walking the rivers of the avenues
feeling the shudder of the caves beneath the asphalt
watching the lights turn on in the towers
walking as I've walked before
like a man, like a woman, in the city
my visionary anger cleansing my sight
and the detailed perceptions of mercy
flowering from that anger

if I come into a room out of the sharp misty light
and hear them talking a dead language
if they ask me my identity
what can I say but
I am the androgyne
I am the living mind you fail to describe
in your dead language
the lost noun, the verb surviving
only in the infinitive
the letters of my name are written under the lids
of the newborn child

1972

Song

You're wondering if I'm lonely:
OK then, yes, I'm lonely
as a plane rides lonely and level
on its radio beam, aiming
across the Rockies
for the blue-strung aisles
of an airfield on the ocean

You want to ask, am I lonely?
Well, of course, lonely
as a woman driving across country
day after day, leaving behind
mile after mile
little towns she might have stopped
and lived and died in, lonely

If I'm lonely
it must be the loneliness
of waking first, of breathing
dawn's first cold breath on the city
of being the one awake
in a house wrapped in sleep

If I'm lonely
it's with the rowboat ice-fast on the shore
in the last red light of the year
that knows what it is, that knows it's neither
ice nor mud nor winter light
but wood, with a gift for burning

1971

Dialogue

She sits with one hand poised against her head, the
other turning an old ring to the light
for hours our talk has beaten
like rain against the screens
a sense of August and heat-lightning
I get up, go to make tea, come back
we look at each other
then she says (and this is what I live through
over and over)—she says: *I do not know*
if sex is an illusion

I do not know
who I was when I did those things
or who I said I was
or whether I willed to feel
what I had read about
or who in fact was there with me
or whether I knew, even then
that there was doubt about these things

1972

Diving into the Wreck

First having read the book of myths,
and loaded the camera,
and checked the edge of the knife-blade,
I put on
the body-armor of black rubber
the absurd flippers
the grave and awkward mask.
I am having to do this
not like Cousteau with his
assiduous team
aboard the sun-flooded schooner
but here alone.

There is a ladder.
The ladder is always there
hanging innocently
close to the side of the schooner.
We know what it is for,
we who have used it.
Otherwise
it's a piece of maritime floss
some sundry equipment.

I go down.
Rung after rung and still
the oxygen immerses me
the blue light
the clear atoms
of our human air.
I go down.
My flippers cripple me,
I crawl like an insect down the ladder

and there is no one
to tell me when the ocean
will begin.

First the air is blue and then
it is bluer and then green and then
black I am blacking out and yet
my mask is powerful
it pumps my blood with power
the sea is another story
the sea is not a question of power
I have to learn alone
to turn my body without force
in the deep element.

And now: it is easy to forget
what I came for
among so many who have always
lived here
swaying their crenellated fans
between the reefs
and besides
you breathe differently down here.

I came to explore the wreck.
The words are purposes.
The words are maps.
I came to see the damage that was done
and the treasures that prevail.
I stroke the beam of my lamp
slowly along the flank
of something more permanent
than fish or weed

the thing I came for:
the wreck and not the story of the wreck
the thing itself and not the myth

the drowned face always staring
toward the sun
the evidence of damage
worn by salt and sway into this threadbare beauty
the ribs of the disaster
curving their assertion
among the tentative haunters.

This is the place.
And I am here, the mermaid whose dark hair
streams black, the merman in his armored body
We circle silently
about the wreck
we dive into the hold.
I am she: I am he

whose drowned face sleeps with open eyes
whose breasts still bear the stress
whose silver, copper, vermeil cargo lies
obscurely inside barrels
half-wedged and left to rot
we are the half-destroyed instruments
that once held to a course
the water-eaten log
the fouled compass

We are, I am, you are
by cowardice or courage
the one who find our way
back to this scene
carrying a knife, a camera
a book of myths
in which
our names do not appear.

1972

II

The Phenomenology of Anger

The Phenomenology of Anger

1. The freedom of the wholly mad
to smear & play with her madness
write with her fingers dipped in it
the length of a room

which is not, of course, the freedom
you have, walking on Broadway
to stop & turn back or go on
10 blocks; 20 blocks

but feels enviable maybe
to the compromised

curled in the placenta of the real
which was to feed & which is strangling her.

2. Trying to light a log that's lain in the damp
as long as this house has stood:
even with dry sticks I can't get started
even with thorns.
I twist last year into a knot of old headlines
—this rose won't bloom.

How does a pile of rags the machinist wiped his hands on
feel in its cupboard, hour upon hour?
Each day during the heat-wave
they took the temperature of the haymow.
I huddled fugitive
in the warm sweet simmer of the hay

muttering: *Come.*

3. Flat heartland of winter.
The moonmen come back from the moon

the firemen come out of the fire.
Time without a taste: time without decisions.

Self-hatred, a monotone in the mind.
The shallowness of a life lived in exile
even in the hot countries.
Cleaver, staring into a window full of knives.

4.   White light splits the room.
Table.   Window.   Lampshade.   You.

My hands, sticky in a new way.
Menstrual blood
seeming to leak from your side.

Will the judges try to tell me
which was the blood of whom?

5.   Madness.   Suicide.   Murder.
Is there no way out but these?
The enemy, always just out of sight
snowshoeing the next forest, shrouded
in a snowy blur, abominable snowman
—at once the most destructive
and the most elusive being
gunning down the babies at My Lai
vanishing in the face of confrontation.

The prince of air and darkness
computing body counts, masturbating
in the factory
of facts.

6.   Fantasies of murder: not enough:
to kill is to cut off from pain
but the killer goes on hurting

Not enough. When I dream of meeting
the enemy, this is my dream:

white acetylene
ripples from my body
effortlessly released
perfectly trained
on the true enemy

raking his body down to the thread
of existence
burning away his lie
leaving him in a new
world; a changed
man

7.   I suddenly see the world
as no longer viable:
you are out there burning the crops
with some new sublimate
This morning you left the bed
we still share
and went out to spread impotence
upon the world

I hate you.
I hate the mask you wear, your eyes
assuming a depth
they do not possess, drawing me
into the grotto of your skull
the landscape of bone
I hate your words
they make me think of fake
revolutionary bills
crisp imitation parchment
they sell at battlefields.

Last night, in this room, weeping
I asked you: *what are you feeling?
do you feel anything?*

Now in the torsion of your body
as you defoliate the fields we lived from
I have your answer.

8.   Dogeared earth. Wormeaten moon.
A pale cross-hatching of silver
lies like a wire screen on the black
water. All these phenomena
are temporary.

I would have loved to live in a world
of women and men gaily
in collusion with green leaves, stalks,
building mineral cities, transparent domes,
little huts of woven grass
each with its own pattern—
a conspiracy to coexist
with the Crab Nebula, the exploding
universe, the Mind—

9.   "The only real love I have ever felt
was for children and other women.
Everything else was lust, pity,
self-hatred, pity, lust."
This is a woman's confession.
Now, look again at the face
of Botticelli's Venus, Kali,
the Judith of Chartres
with her so-called smile.

10. how we are burning up our lives
testimony:
>the subway
>hurtling to Brooklyn
>her head on her knees
>asleep or drugged

la vía del tren subterráneo
es peligrosa
>many sleep
>the whole way

>others sit
>staring holes of fire into the air

>others plan rebellion:
>night after night
>awake in prison, my mind
>licked at the mattress like a flame
>till the cellblock went up roaring

>Thoreau setting fire to the woods

Every act of becoming conscious
(it says here in this book)
is an unnatural act

1972

III

I saw a beggar leaning on his crutch,
He said to me: Why do you ask for so much?
I saw a woman leaning in a door,
She said, Why not, why not, why not ask for more?

—*Leonard Cohen's "Bird on a Wire"*
(*as sung by Judy Collins*)

Merced

Fantasies of old age:
they have rounded us up
in a rest-camp for the outworn.
Somewhere in some dustbowl
a barbed-wire cantonment
of low-cost dustcolored prefab
buildings, smelling of shame
and hopeless incontinence
identical clothes of disposable
paper, identical rations
of chemically flavored food
Death in order, by gas,
hypodermics daily
to neutralize despair
So I imagine my world
in my seventieth year alive
and outside the barbed wire
a purposeless exchange
of consciousness for the absence
of pain. We will call this life.

Yet only last summer I
burned my feet in the sand
of that valley traced by the thread
of the cold quick river Merced
watered by plummets of white
When I swam, my body ached
from the righteous cold
when I lay back floating the jays
flittered from pine to pine
and the shade moved hour by hour

across El Capitan
Our wine cooled in the water
and I watched my sons, half-men
half-children, testing their part
in a world almost archaic
so precious by this time
that merely to step in pure water
or stare into clear air
is to feel a spasm of pain.

For weeks now a rage
has possessed my body, driving
now out upon men and women
now inward upon myself
Walking Amsterdam Avenue
I find myself in tears
without knowing which thought
forced water to my eyes
To speak to another human
becomes a risk
I think of Norman Morrison
the Buddhists of Saigon
the black teacher last week
who put himself to death
to waken guilt in hearts
too numb to get the message
in a world masculinity made
unfit for women or men
Taking off in a plane
I look down at the city
which meant life to me, not death
and think that somewhere there
a cold center, composed

of pieces of human beings
metabolized, restructured
by a process they do not feel
is spreading in our midst
and taking over our minds
a thing that feels neither guilt
nor rage: that is unable
to hate, therefore to love.

1972

A Primary Ground

"But he must have more than that. It was sympathy he wanted, to be assured of his genius, first of all, and then to be taken within the circle of life, warmed and soothed, to have his sense restored to him, his barrenness made fertile, and all the rooms of the house made full of life . . ."
                                            —*Virginia Woolf, To the Lighthouse*

And this is how you live: a woman, children
protect you from the abyss
you move near, turning on the news
eating Thanksgiving with its pumpkin teeth
drinking the last wine
from the cellar of your wedding

It all seems innocent enough, this sin
of wedlock: you, your wife, your children
leaning across the unfilled plates
passing the salt
down a cloth ironed by a woman
with aching legs
Now they go out to play
in the coarse, rough November air
that smells of soft-coal smoke, the river,
burnt sweet-potato pie.

Sensuality dessicates in words—
risks of the portage, risks of the glacier
never taken
Protection is the genius of your house
the pressure of the steam iron
flattens the linen cloth again
chestnuts puréed with care are dutifully eaten

in every room the furniture reflects you
larger than life, or dwindling

Emptiness
thrust like a batch of letters to the furthest
dark of a drawer
But there is something else:
your wife's twin sister, speechless
is dying in the house
You and your wife take turns
carrying up the trays,
understanding her case, trying to make her understand.

1972

Translations

You show me the poems of some woman
my age, or younger
translated from your language

Certain words occur: *enemy, oven, sorrow*
enough to let me know
she's a woman of my time

obsessed

with Love, our subject:
we've trained it like ivy to our walls
baked it like bread in our ovens
worn it like lead on our ankles
watched it through binoculars as if
it were a helicopter
bringing food to our famine
or the satellite
of a hostile power

I begin to see that woman
doing things: stirring rice
ironing a skirt
typing a manuscript till dawn

trying to make a call
from a phonebooth

The phone rings unanswered
in a man's bedroom
she hears him telling someone else
Never mind. She'll get tired.
hears him telling her story to her sister

who becomes her enemy
and will in her own time
light her own way to sorrow

ignorant of the fact this way of grief
is shared, unnecessary
and political

1972

in spirit,
co-authoress:
D. Fox JAKOB

Living in the Cave

Reading the Parable of the Cave
while living in the cave,

                  black moss

deadening my footsteps
candles stuck on rock-ledges
weakening my eyes

These things around me, with their
daily requirements:

                fill me, empty me
talk to me, warm me, let me
suck on you

Every one of them has a plan that depends on me

stalactites want to become
stalagmites
veins of ore
imagine their preciousness

candles see themselves disembodied
into gas
and taking flight

the bat hangs dreaming
of an airy world

None of them, not one
sees me
as I see them

1972

The Ninth Symphony
of Beethoven Understood At Last
As a Sexual Message

A man in terror of impotence
or infertility, not knowing the difference
a man trying to tell something
howling from the climacteric
music of the entirely
isolated soul
yelling at Joy from the tunnel of the ego
music without the ghost
of another person in it, music
trying to tell something the man
does not want out, would keep if he could
gagged and bound and flogged with chords of Joy
where everything is silence and the
beating of a bloody fist upon
a splintered table

1972

Rape

There is a cop who is both prowler and father:
he comes from your block, grew up with your brothers,
had certain ideals.
You hardly know him in his boots and silver badge,
on horseback, one hand touching his gun.

You hardly know him but you have to get to know him:
he has access to machinery that could kill you.
He and his stallion clop like warlords among the trash,
his ideals stand in the air, a frozen cloud
from between his unsmiling lips.

And so, when the time comes, you have to turn to him,
the maniac's sperm still greasing your thighs,
your mind whirling like crazy. You have to confess
to him, you are guilty of the crime
of having been forced.

And you see his blue eyes, the blue eyes of all the family
whom you used to know, grow narrow and glisten,
his hand types out the details
and he wants them all
but the hysteria in your voice pleases him best.

You hardly know him but now he thinks he knows you:
he has taken down your worst moment
on a machine and filed it in a file.
He knows, or thinks he knows, how much you imagined;
he knows, or thinks he knows, what you secretly wanted.

He has access to machinery that could get you put away;
and if, in the sickening light of the precinct,
and if, in the sickening light of the precinct,
your details sound like a portrait of your confessor,
will you swallow, will you deny them. will you lie your way home?

1972

Burning Oneself In

In a bookstore on the East Side
I read a veteran's testimony:

the running down, for no reason
of an old woman in South Vietnam
by a U.S. Army truck

The heat-wave is over
Lifeless, sunny, the East Side
rests under its awnings

Another summer
The flames go on feeding

and a dull heat permeates the ground
of the mind, the burn has settled in
as if it had no more question

of its right to go on devouring
the rest of a lifetime,
the rest of history

Pieces of information, like this one
blow onto the heap

they keep it fed, whether we will it or not,
another summer, and another
of suffering quietly

in bookstores, in the parks
however we may scream we are
suffering quietly

1972

Burning Oneself Out

(*for E. K.*

We can look into the stove tonight
as into a mirror, yes,

the serrated log, the yellow-blue
gaseous core

the crimson-flittered grey ash, yes,
I know inside my eyelids
and underneath my skin

Time takes hold of us like a draft
upward, drawing at the heats
in the belly, in the brain

You told me of setting your hand
into the print of a long-dead Indian
and for a moment, I knew that hand,

that print, that rock,
that sun producing powerful dreams
A word can do this

or, as tonight, the mirror of the fire
of my mind, burning as if it could go on
burning itself, burning down

feeding on everything
till there is nothing in life
that has not fed that fire

1972

For a Sister

(Natalya Gorbanevskaya, two years in-carcerated in a Soviet penal mental asylum for her political activism; and others

I trust none of them. Only my existence
thrown out in the world like a towchain
battered and twisted in many chance connections,
being pulled this way, pulling in that.

I have to steal the sense of dust on your floor,
milk souring in your pantry
after they came and took you.
I'm forced to guess at the look you threw backward.

A few paragraphs in the papers,
allowing for printers' errors, wilful omissions,
the trained violence of doctors.
I don't trust them, but I'm learning how to use them.

Little by little out of the blurred conjectures
your face clears, a sunken marble
slowly cranked up from underwater.
I feel the ropes straining under their load of despair.

They searched you for contraband, they made their notations.
A look of intelligence could get you twenty years.
Better to trace nonexistent circles with your finger,
try to imitate the smile of the permanently dulled.

My images. This metaphor for what happens.
A geranium in flames on a green cloth
becomes yours. You, coming home after years
to light the stove, get out the typewriter and begin again. Your story.

1972

For the Dead

I dreamed I called you on the telephone
to say: *Be kinder to yourself*
but you were sick and would not answer

The waste of my love goes on this way
trying to save you from yourself

I have always wondered about the leftover
energy, water rushing down a hill
long after the rains have stopped

or the fire you want to go to bed from
but cannot leave, burning-down but not burnt-down
the red coals more extreme, more curious
in their flashing and dying
than you wish they were
sitting there long after midnight

1972

From a Survivor

The pact that we made was the ordinary pact
of men & women in those days

I don't know who we thought we were
that our personalities
could resist the failures of the race

Lucky or unlucky, we didn't know
the race had failures of that order
and that we were going to share them

Like everybody else, we thought of ourselves as special

Your body is as vivid to me
as it ever was: even more

since my feeling for it is clearer:
I know what it could do and could not do

it is no longer
the body of a god
or anything with power over my life

Next year it would have been 20 years
and you are wastefully dead
who might have made the leap
we talked, too late, of making

which I live now
not as a leap
but a succession of brief, amazing movements

each one making possible the next

1972

August

Two horses in yellow light
eating windfall apples under a tree

as summer tears apart   milkweeds stagger
and grasses grow more ragged

They say there are ions in the sun
neutralizing magnetic fields on earth

Some way to explain
what this week has been, and the one before it!

If I am flesh sunning on rock
if I am brain burning in fluorescent light

if I am dream like a wire with fire
throbbing along it

if I am death to man
I have to know it

His mind is too simple, I cannot go on
sharing his nightmares

My own are becoming clearer, they open
into prehistory

which looks like a village lit with blood
where all the fathers are crying: *My son is mine!*

1972

IV

Meditations for a Savage Child

Meditations
for a Savage Child

*(The prose passages are from
J-M Itard's account of* The Wild
Boy of Aveyron, *as translated by
G. and M. Humphrey)*

I

*There was a profound indifference to the objects of our plea-
sures and of our fictitious needs; there was still . . . so in-
tense a passion for the freedom of the fields . . . that he
would certainly have escaped into the forest had not the most
rigid precautions been taken . . .*

In their own way, by their own lights
they tried to care for you
tried to teach you to care
for objects of their caring:

        glossed oak planks, glass
        whirled in a fire
        to impossible thinness

to teach you names
for things
you did not need

        muslin shirred against the sun
        linen on a sack of feathers
        locks, keys
        boxes with coins inside

they tried to make you feel
the importance of

                    a piece of cowhide
                    sewn around a bundle
                    of leaves impressed with signs

to teach you language:
the thread their lives
were strung on

II

When considered from a more general and philosophic point of view, these scars bear witness . . . against the feebleness and insufficiency of man when left entirely to himself, and in favor of the resources of nature which . . . work openly to repair and conserve that which she tends secretly to impair and destroy.

I keep thinking about the lesson of the human ear
which stands for music, which stands for balance—
or the cat's ear which I can study better
the whorls and ridges exposed
It seems a hint dropped about the inside of the skull
which I cannot see
lobe, zone, that part of the brain
which is pure survival

The most primitive part
I go back into at night
pushing the leathern curtain
with naked fingers
then
with naked body

There where every wound is registered
as scar tissue

A cave of scars!
ancient, archaic wallpaper
built up, layer on layer
from the earliest, dream-white

to yesterday's, a red-black scrawl
a red mouth slowly closing

Go back so far there is another language
go back far enough the language
is no longer personal

these scars bear witness
but whether to repair
or to destruction
I no longer know

III

*It is true that there is visible on the throat a very extended
scar which might throw some doubt upon the soundness of
the underlying parts if one were not reassured by the appear-
ance of the scar . . .*

When I try to speak
my throat is cut
and, it seems, by his hand

The sounds I make are prehuman, radical
the telephone is always
ripped-out

and he sleeps on
Yet always the tissue
grows over, white as silk

hardly a blemish
maybe a hieroglyph for scream

Child, no wonder you never wholly
trusted your keepers

IV

*A hand with the will rather than the habit of crime had wished
to make an attempt on the life of this child . . . left for dead
in the woods, he will have owed the prompt recovery of his
wound to the help of nature alone.*

In the 18th century infanticide
reaches epidemic proportions:
old prints attest to it: starving mothers
smothering babies in sleep
abandoning newborns in sleet
on the poorhouse steps
gin-blurred, setting fire to the room

I keep thinking of the flights we used to take
on the grapevine across the gully
littered with beer-bottles where dragonflies flashed
we were 10, 11 years old
wild little girls with boyish bodies
flying over the moist
shadow-mottled earth
till they warned us to stay away from there

Later they pointed out
the venetian blinds
of the abortionist's house
we shivered

Men can do things to you
was all they said

V

*And finally, my Lord, looking at this long experiment . . .
whether it be considered as the methodical education of a
savage or as no more than the physical and moral treatment
of one of those creatures ill-favored by nature, rejected by so-
ciety and abandoned by medicine, the care that has been taken
and ought still to be taken of him, the changes that have taken
place, and those that can be hoped for, the voice of humanity,
the interest inspired by such a desertion and a destiny so
strange—all these things recommend this extraordinary young
man to the attention of scientists, to the solicitude of admin-
istrators, and to the protection of the government.*

1. The doctor in "Uncle Vanya":
   *They will call us fools,
   blind, ignorant, they will
   despise us*

   devourers of the forest
   leaving teeth of metal in every tree
   so the tree can neither grow
   nor be cut for lumber

   Does the primeval forest
   weep
   for its devourers

   does nature mourn
   our existence

is the child with arms
burnt to the flesh of its sides
weeping eyelessly for man

2. At the end of the distinguished doctor's
    lecture
    a young woman raises her hand:

    You have the power
    in your hands, you control our lives—
    why do you want our pity too?

    Why are men afraid
    why do you pity yourselves
    why do the administrators

    lack solicitude, the government
    refuse protection,

    why should the wild child
    weep for the scientists

    why